# *Listen to Your Heart*
## *guided journal*

Daily journal prompts for personal growth and self discovery so you can find out what makes you happy in 30 days.

A Soul Scroll Journal

By Suzanne Heyn

*Understand yourself to create a life*
*as unique as you are.*

For bonus resources visit:
SoulScrollJournals.com/bonuses

DISCLAIMER

This book is for entertainment purposes only. This journal is not a substitute for therapy or professional medical or mental health advice.

Although the Author has made every effort to ensure the information in this book was correct at press time, the author does not assume and hereby disclaims any liability to any part for any loss, damage, or disruption caused by this book.

The Author and/or distributors are not responsible for any adverse effects resulting from the use of the suggestions outlined in this program.

# Table of contents

# Welcome!

Congratulations on investing in yourself in both time and money to create positive shifts in your life! The intention of this journal is to help you listen to your heart, find out exactly what you want and connect to the inner guidance to mold your every day into something beautiful.

Sometimes we feel lost, uncertain or held back by circumstances that seem beyond our control. Maybe you have no idea what you want, or know, but aren't sure how to create it.

In either case, this guided journal will support you to find clarity, connect to your higher self and start creating positive changes in your life today.

The good news is that times of frustration or uncertainty are actually powerful thresholds inviting you to step into a new level of yourself and life.

Here's what I know for sure: You are powerful beyond measure. You are exactly where you're supposed to be and who you're supposed to be.

You have everything you need to design a life you love, a life as unique as you are. It's all inside of you. This is true even if it feels like you're trapped or nothing is working in your favor — especially then.

During the coming days and weeks, you'll learn exactly how to create the necessary mindset shifts to find doorways where before there were only walls. You'll learn how to become the person you've always known you could be.

An infinite intelligence is always moving through you, guiding you to a life you love. The more faith you place in this intelligence, and the more consciously you spend time connecting to it, the more life will expand beyond your wildest dreams.

Things can happen fast when you allow yourself to trust life and surrender into the unknown.

Throughout this journal, I share tools and beliefs that helped me listen to my heart even when I felt stuck and sad, like I was living somebody else's life. Answering these questions helped me expand into an experience of knowing who I am, what I want and exactly how to create it.

These shifts helped me create more fulfilling, balanced relationships. Rather than sacrificing my needs and desires, I now know I deserve to receive as much as I give.

These tools helped me discover my purpose and make a living with my truest gifts. They helped me understand what I really wanted and the life I longed to live rather than what others expected from me or what looked cool on social media.

This is what I want to help you experience, too. But while I share the beliefs, tools and mindset shifts I found useful, my highest intention is to help you tap into what's true for you.

This is a time for you to listen to your heart, away from the opinions of gurus, family, friends and society, so you can hear your inner voice.

It's time to stop idolizing others and start idolizing yourself.

Self-awareness created through self-inquiry is the most powerful tool for change there is. (As long as it's followed by action!)

With that in mind, a word of caution: It's said that the observer influences the outcome of the experiment.

That's why it's very important to be aware of when you're subconsciously responding in this journal from a place of writing what you think other people (including me) would want you to say.

I know you don't know me, but our desire for approval and to fit in is so strong that sometimes it's hard to fully drop that.

These next 30 days are about dropping all layers and connecting to who you really are. You're about to shed everything standing between you and your extraordinary life — not because you're not good enough as you are, but because you are so beyond good enough and deserve everything you dream of.

Know that. This work is everything.

**To introduce myself, my name is Suzanne Heyn, and I am the founder of Soul Scroll Journals.**

I am committed to helping people understand themselves so they can create lives as unique as they are.

There was a time I was so focused on following the rules and what I thought I should be doing that I lost the connection to my heart, to what I really wanted.

I've found that underneath this disconnection were fears about whether my dreams were possible, or whether I'd be worthy of love if I lived them out.

If this resonates, you're in the right place. I know how to release those stories, along with any past pain keeping you stuck in them, so you can free yourself and follow your heart to create a life as unique as you are.

Journaling is a powerful tool for creating a life fueled by hope and faith rather than one limited by past pain and fear.

More recently, along the path of realizing my dreams, I followed what's become the conventional, unconventional path — starting a blog and monetizing with coaching and courses.

Over time, this stopped feeling fulfilling. Because I didn't trust my inner voice and felt terrified that shifting what I was doing meant giving up on my dreams all together, I didn't ask myself the questions necessary to grow.

But one day, the frustration mounted, inspiring me to ask a question that ushered in an unbelievable sense of freedom: What would I do if I wasn't doing this?

It sounds simple, but sometimes we don't give ourselves the freedom to ask these questions because old stories, fears or limiting beliefs keep us walking in the same old circles.

Through asking that question, I eventually received the vision to create a series of journals like this one, along with an electric surge of excitement letting me know this was the right path.

It felt scary to shift away from the things I'd worked so hard to create to start something new, but that's why trusting ourselves is essential for creating a life as unique as we are. (And identifying the reasons we don't trust ourselves so we can move beyond them.)

It's my intention that this story show the power of giving ourselves permission to ask fresh questions. To allow ourselves to start again, and to show that times of turmoil or stagnation are turning points, not dead ends.

The right questions mark the difference between happiness and sadness, between feeling empowered or stuck, and the difference between a life well lived versus one ending in regret.

The right questions can and will change your life, and that's why I'm so excited for you to experience this journal.

Nobody will ever understand you the way you understand yourself, and sadly most people don't understand themselves at all. Self-awareness is the foundation to happiness.

So get ready. Dig deep. Do more than you feel ready for. You are capable of much more than you likely allow yourself to believe.

Happy soul scrolling!


All the love,

*Suzanne Heyn*

Founder, Soul Scroll Journals


PS — Share your journaling experience on social media tagging #soulscrolling or @soulscrolljournals for the chance to be featured!


PPS — Add a daily meditation practice to your 30-day journaling experience. On SoulScrollJournals.com/bonuses, you'll find a free, super powerful meditation for connecting to your heart and releasing any stuck emotions blocking you from hearing its wisdom.

## How to use this journal

It's best to carve out time each day to read the day's passage and journal your thoughts. This could make a wonderful morning or evening practice.

However, this journey is ultimately yours to do however feels aligned to your best interest. What's important is that you make it a priority, intentionally carving time out for it. If you skip a day or a few days, return to the work quickly.

It's easy to start with sky-high intentions, but you'll be facing things that feel difficult or even scary. You will stir things up that have sat dormant for a long time.

It's natural for resistance to show up, and sometimes resistance likes to convince you that scrolling your phone or watching tv is more important than scrolling your soul!

Show up for yourself. Creating change isn't about consuming information. It's about going within and seeing where perspectives and pains that don't serve you are controlling your life. The time has come to release them.

You are about to create powerful shifts that will forever change your life! The woman you are becoming thanks you for this. Take a moment, and write out an intention. Why is doing this work important to you? What are you ready to create?

_____

_____

_____

_____

*Bonus resources*

### Free meditation for releasing painful emotions

As you connect to your heart, things come up. Head to SoulScrollJournals.com/bonuses to access your free meditation to process what you feel and connect to your inner wisdom.

### Join the Soul Scroll Journals Family Facebook group!

Personal growth can be lonely, but it doesn't have to be! Head to www.facebook.com/groups/soulscrolljournals to connect with others on the path of creating a unique, soulful life.

# Week 1: Radical honesty

Awareness is the first step to creating change.

You can't change something without first getting honest about how things are and setting clear intentions for how you want to shift.

Adopt an approach of curiosity and compassion rather than criticism and judgment. Be gentle, but honest. Lying to yourself hurts no one but you.

# Day 1: Get it out!

It's time to get really, really real with yourself. In order to create change in your life, it's important to first become aware of everything you're tired of.

Today is about writing down all the things you're done with to erase them from your head with the intention of wiping the slate clean.

It's time to create change.

Keep in mind that you can't control external situations or other people. All you can control is you: what you do, how you show up in life, and how you respond to situations.

Everything begins with a shift in perspective, which will lead to changes in how you interact with life, but today we are creating awareness, space and intentional focus.

So today, write down what you no longer want to do. The ways you're letting yourself down or breaking promises to yourself. The things you've been doing that don't become you, that don't represent the person you know you can be.

This might involve work, relationships, fitness, areas where you're not fully showing up for yourself, not creating or enforcing boundaries, or even simply admitting that you're lost and you don't know what's next.

Ask: What are you tired of? What parts of you have fallen asleep? Where have you been meaning to make changes, but have wavered in your commitment?

This is NOT about beating yourself up, but instead becoming aware and getting to a place of decision.

Today is about deciding that you're ready for change and will do what's required. You are now, today, deciding that you are creating a different kind of life.

It's time to get soul naked so you can shift. Dump it all out. Let it all go. Too many people are focused on being overly positive (or avoidant) and never allow themselves space to sort through their inner shit.

There's gold in there. Let's find it.

After you're done, write a declaration of what you want or believe is possible. Something like, "I am ready to release all that no longer serves me. Thank you Universe. I am ready for something new. Please show me the way."

------------------------------------------------

------------------------------------------------

------------------------------------------------

------------------------------------------------

------------------------------------------------

------------------------------------------------

------------------------------------------------

------------------------------------------------

------------------------------------------------

------------------------------------------------

------------------------------------------------

------------------------------------------------

------------------------------------------------

------------------------------------------------

------------------------------------------------

# Day 2: Identify your resistance.

Today is about identifying the areas of life you're fighting along with the underlying fears causing you to fight. In life, we're either contracting or expanding, moving from fear or love. It's natural to move from fear sometimes. We're only human!

But creating a unique, soulful life requires us to become aware of our deeper fears and insecurities so we can understand how they cause us to fight rather than flow.

You can't hear your heart or use life energy for creation if you're fighting the flow of life or fighting what is. Trust that no matter what your life looks like right now, you have everything you need to take the next step toward the life you want.

Listening to your heart and creating a beautiful life is about taking one next right step at a time. What's required is to trust, stay grateful and move from faith. To do that, it's important to identify and honor your fears! So let's dive in.

One of the most common reasons people fight what is rather than focus on what they want is because they fear their desires aren't possible. A sense of powerlessness may accompany this fear.

The first step to reclaiming your power is to accept that you feel powerless, which is the fear that your situation is unchangeable. Accepting this fear leads to accepting your circumstances which leads to receiving inspired guidance for how to move forward based on how things are, rather than how you wish they were.

To do this, open up to the feeling of fear in your body. Breathe into it rather than resist it. Let this fear speak. Identify the stories you're telling yourself about why you're stuck or can't move forward so you can write new, more empowering stories.

Whatever comes up, surrender to it. Write everything down. Don't worry if something feels true; that doesn't mean that it is.

Another reason people fight what is are fears that wrong decisions or painful past experiences have made it impossible to live a life they love. Know there's ultimately no right or wrong decision. Everything is either a lesson or a blessing. No matter what the past has held, you can create something beautiful. And no matter where you are, you can always create something new.

A third common fear is people feeling like they won't be worthy of love if they get what they want. This is common with career and love choices. For example, maybe your family or friends don't agree with a certain choice, and you feel like you can't do what you want.

Maybe your parents sacrificed for you, or paid for your schooling, or believed that a "respectable" child does or doesn't behave in certain ways. A feeling of guilt can stop you from following your heart.

Today dig deeper. Why do you feel like you can't do what you want? Why do you feel like you have to listen to other people over your own heart? Begin to question everything you think rather than blindly believing it.

Another common type of resistance is feeling that because you don't have something you want, you're not worthy of it.

This one is tricky because often we feel like we need this thing — a job, to make a certain amount of money, for our body to look a certain way or to have a certain relationship — to be worthy. The fact that we don't have it seems to prove that we don't deserve it!

Ironically, this feeling of unworthiness blocks us from receiving the thing we want. There are a lot of layers to healing this, but today's work is simply about identifying any stories locking you in this quagmire.

Another scenario is that perhaps life has delivered unexpected, unwelcome circumstances and you have fears around what they mean or how you'll make it through. Trust that you can and you will. Trust that you can create something beautiful from anything.

This is your invitation to reinvent yourself, to expand, to dream a new dream or believe in an old dream more fully. Whatever is, is supposed to be. Otherwise it wouldn't be.

In either case, it is what it is. This is what you have to work with! Might as well embrace it so you can create magic. It's all possible. But first you have to believe. You have to open your heart to yourself and to life so you can receive the guidance that will help you move forward.

There is a big, wonderful plan for your life. You are meant for extraordinary things. All that's standing in your way is the fear that's not true.

Today ask: What are you fighting in life and why? Where are you holding on, wishing something was different than it is?

What are you afraid not having this thing says about who you are or what's possible? How can you see these things differently?

_____

_____

------------------------------------------------------------
------------------------------------------------------------
------------------------------------------------------------
------------------------------------------------------------
------------------------------------------------------------
------------------------------------------------------------
------------------------------------------------------------
------------------------------------------------------------
------------------------------------------------------------
------------------------------------------------------------
------------------------------------------------------------
------------------------------------------------------------
------------------------------------------------------------
------------------------------------------------------------
------------------------------------------------------------
------------------------------------------------------------
------------------------------------------------------------
------------------------------------------------------------
------------------------------------------------------------
------------------------------------------------------------
------------------------------------------------------------
------------------------------------------------------------
------------------------------------------------------------
------------------------------------------------------------
------------------------------------------------------------
------------------------------------------------------------
------------------------------------------------------------

# Day 3: Identify old stories you no longer need.

Humans are driven by story. We're the main characters in the epic tales of our lives, with hopes and dreams and fears, but also conflicts and challenges that must be overcome along the way.

Sometimes it's not an event or situation that causes pain, but the meaning we attach to it. The story we tell ourselves about it.

Maybe you're telling stories that because something in your past has happened, you can't create the future you want. Or because some health issue, mental pattern or money trouble has manifested in your family for generations, you're also doomed to struggle with it.

Maybe you have a story that says you have to work a certain type of job or achieve some arbitrary goal to be good enough, and you feel stuck trying to force things, afraid to let go and flow.

Whenever we're in a place of emotional or mental angst, chances are an outdated story is running the show: "It's not safe to follow my heart." "I'm not good enough." "I can't." "People will be disappointed in me if I do what I really want."

These negative stories are understandably scary, heavy and sad. They're also not true. They're keeping you stuck. It's time to release these old stories and tell life-affirming new ones.

Most of these stories don't even come from us, but are the voices of other people — parents, teachers, even someone you look up to — that have infiltrated our inner voice.

Maybe you experienced a failure or disappointment, and the story around this is you're not good enough, don't have what it takes, or will never be successful.

Maybe you encountered a breakup and are having a hard time letting go because you're telling a story that you're not lovable.

Maybe you're not sure what you want in life, and are creating a story that you're powerless, can't create change, and don't know what you want. (Your heart always knows what you want! The story you no longer need is whatever one that's blocking connection to your inner voice.)

Today, consider the thing you're struggling with the most. What stories are you telling about this thing, your own abilities, or what's required of you?

Keep writing until you feel a sense of completion. If you run out of things to write, but don't feel that sense of completion, simply ask, "What else?"

Then, ask yourself if these stories are true. (If it doesn't feel good, it's not true.)

Finally, write a new story. What would you rather believe instead? Connect to your heart and ask for guidance from your higher self by simply setting the intention and seeing what message comes up. (Trust yourself!) If you ever feel like you don't know, ask, "If I did know, what would the answer be?"

Some ideas for new stories include:

I can create anything I want to.

Because an idea was placed in my heart, it's mine to create. I believe it's my time to prosper, expand and grow. I am ready to love myself and believe in myself more deeply. I can create anything I want from exactly where I am.

I am ready to become the confident, carefree, successful and abundant woman I know I already am deep inside. I am ready to let my true self shine and become who I was born to be.

_____

_____

_____

_____

_____

_____

_____

_____

_____

_____

_____

_____

_____

_____

_____

_____

_____

_____

_____

_____

_____

_____

# Day 4: Who do you think you are?

How is your definition of yourself — anything that follows, "I am," — influencing you?

Adding onto yesterday's exploration of the stories we tell ourselves, a lot of times we move through our lives as actors playing roles rather than as who we truly want to be.

You may very well be a mother / father / wife / husband / daughter / son / employee / boss, but feel trapped in what you think those roles require.

"If I'm a mom, it's selfish to take time to myself." "My parents expect me to work a certain type of job, and they sacrificed a lot for me. It's selfish to disappoint them and follow my heart."

"Good employees say yes to every request, eat lunch at their desk, and never take vacation."

"Good daughters aren't allowed to set boundaries with parents even if the relationship feels draining or toxic."

These are all lies that leak your energy and make you unhappy. They keep you from following your dreams. You get to decide how you want to show up in the relationships and roles that matter to you.

These stories are often deep-rooted in ideas about what's required to be good enough or worthy of love or even just to fit in. It can feel scary to stand out, but darling you were born to shine!

Once you find the courage to follow your heart and be who you want to be, you will feel so good. You feeling good is in the highest good for all.

Trust that you're a good person, and that by following your heart and honoring your desires, you can fulfill your responsibilities from a place of joyful service. We, in our natural state, naturally want to support others and do an amazing job.

Rather than being selfish to do your own thing or put yourself first, it's selfish not to. Happiness comes from living lives that are true to us, and happy people spread joy and change the world.

We are alive to follow our joy and fill our lives with things that make us happy. That's ultimately what this journey is about — recognizing your true nature and creating a life as unique as you are. Your pure, unfiltered essence is an incredible gift to the world.

So let's dive in.

First, write down all the roles you play or ways you describe yourself. (Feel free to focus on one thing if that feels overwhelming.)

Second, ask: What do you think is required for those roles?

Third, ask: Which of those requirements does not feel good?

Fourth, ask: What would it mean to show up for the things that are important to me, in a way that feels really good?

And fifth, if necessary, ask: What do I need to know to give myself permission to do what I want? Tap into your higher self for guidance if you're not sure how to shift.

Notice any limiting ideas that come up. "Oh I could never ask so and so to help with that. He would just say no!" The truth is, you have a certain idea of the roles you're expected to play and are in relationships with others who likely have those same expectations. This is only showing you what you've tolerated, and in doing so, created situations and dynamics that drain your energy and cause you to feel resentful. It's time to speak up for yourself kindly but firmly and find solutions of the highest good.

The people who truly love you want to support you. This honest communication will only deepen your relationships. It is safe to follow your heart.

# Day 5: Give your inner conflicts a voice.

Today is about giving all of you space to express how you think and feel. Yesterday we examined the roles you play and what you think is required to be good at them. Wanting to be good enough or worthy drives many of our decisions.

Also driving our decisions, or rather indecision, are inner conflicts. This is when one part of us wants something different than another part, or one part of us holds on to the past while another wants to let go.

Moving forward isn't about fighting different parts of yourself, but rather accepting them and finding out what they need to feel safe. This allows your entire being — mind, body, heart and soul — to align with a single intention, amplifying your power and supercharging your forward momentum.

For example, the part of you who wants to feel safe and loved (and likely feels deep down that you must do or not do certain things to be worthy of that love), will create conflict with the part of you who desires certain things, like starting a business, setting a boundary, taking a trip, or following a dream.

The more you do inner work like this, the more you'll understand all parts of you. When you understand yourself totally, you gain the ability to give all parts of you what you need, with compassion.

You'll also understand why you do the things you do, or why change sometimes feels hard to make. A lot of times indecision, procrastination, or deeper feelings of anxiety, sadness or anger relate to these inner conflicts. The noise they create blocks us from hearing our inner guidance.

So today, tune into the different parts of you. What does each wish to say?

An easy way to access this work is to tune into any feelings you're experiencing.

If you feel frustrated, blocked or unfulfilled, what does that emotion want to say?

If you feel overwhelmed, tired or burned out, what does that energy have to say?

If you feel afraid, angry, sad or anxious, what do those emotions have to say?

What does your inner child wish to say?

What does your higher self wish to say?

You could even dialogue with any physical pain or illness you're experiencing. What message does it have for you? What does it want you to know?

This might sound weird, but as soon as you drop in and begin listening, you'll be shocked to see the messages and wisdom flowing from your pen, giving you insights that will change your life.

If at any time you feel stuck, simply ask your higher self / soul / the Universe, whatever resonates with you — What do I need to know to move beyond this?

As a final note, you may find all the voices interrupting each other as you write. An angry or upset voice may interrupt the voice of faith, for example. This is a time to give space for the voices of pain to exist, even if that feels scary. It might, for a moment, feel like you're not making any progress or even moving backwards as fears come up these thoughts and feelings will never go away.

The emotions will release, but first you must create space for them to exist rather than resist them, wishing they weren't there or feeling flawed for feeling them. There's nothing wrong with you.

This work is very important because these are the very conflicts keeping you stuck. Taking the time to air them out is what will allow you to find peace while creating a pathway forward. This is no small thing. Trust the process.

When painful thoughts come up that feel true and you can't see beyond them, ask for guidance.

"What do I need to know that will take me to the other side?" Keep your pen flowing. You got this.

_____

_____

_____

_____

_____

_____

_____

_____

_____

_____

_____

_____

---------------------------------------------------------------

---------------------------------------------------------------

---------------------------------------------------------------

---------------------------------------------------------------

---------------------------------------------------------------

---------------------------------------------------------------

---------------------------------------------------------------

---------------------------------------------------------------

---------------------------------------------------------------

---------------------------------------------------------------

---------------------------------------------------------------

---------------------------------------------------------------

---------------------------------------------------------------

---------------------------------------------------------------

---------------------------------------------------------------

---------------------------------------------------------------

---------------------------------------------------------------

---------------------------------------------------------------

---------------------------------------------------------------

---------------------------------------------------------------

---------------------------------------------------------------

---------------------------------------------------------------

---------------------------------------------------------------

---------------------------------------------------------------

---------------------------------------------------------------

---------------------------------------------------------------

---------------------------------------------------------------

# Day 6: What are you afraid of?

Our problems begin in the mind. Our limited, fearful thoughts, beliefs and perspectives block us from seeing possibilities.

They stop us from taking risks and following our hearts because we believe the fear-based thoughts that mostly aren't true. Creating clarity on your doubts and fears is a powerful way to move beyond them.

When they exist in the mind, they slow you down and appear real. By spilling them out on the paper, you gain the ability to prove them wrong. Sometimes the simple act of writing down your fears is enough to release them.

Whatever you want to create in life, whatever dream or vision is held deep in your heart, it's possible. Fear is the only thing standing in your way.

And yes, often fear shows up as excuses like, "I don't have enough time," "I don't have enough money," "I don't know how," or "It'll happen when the time is right." You have all the resources you need to take the next step. And divine timing is often waiting on us to decide it's time and make the first move!

Two main fears stop us from following our hearts: The fear of not being loved. And the fear of being unsafe, which includes death, poverty and homelessness.

Know there's ultimately nothing to be afraid of. You are inherently lovable because you are. Nothing you do could make you unworthy of love, even failing.

No matter what happens in life, even if you ran out of money, there are always options to create more. You always have a right next step. There is a way up from every bottom.

Meanwhile, contemplating your death can be a powerful motivator to move forward! It's true. You're going to die; you're not going to live forever. You don't know how much time you have. This is your life, and you have to die when it's your time. Thinking about facing that final moment can help you find the courage to live more fully now.

Sometimes coming to peace with our greatest fears, and knowing we'd be okay even if they happened, can help us move beyond them.

Today, start journaling your fears in these main areas and anything else that comes up for you. What are you afraid of? Get it out.

If the fear is potentially true, such as fearing that some people might judge you, ask yourself if it matters. Are you willing to sacrifice your life and your dream for this fear? What matters more to you — your happiness and fulfillment or running away from fear, allowing it to control you? You get to choose.

You are more powerful than anything that could stand in your way. You are resourceful beyond measure. When you put your whole heart and energy behind your desires, and trust that you can find or create everything you need to succeed, unlimited possibilities unravel.

When you allow yourself to connect to the magic of the universe, life becomes magical.

But first, you have to become aware of what's holding you back.

After journaling out your fears, shift to an empowering new story. What would you rather believe? If you're not sure, ask your higher self to help you find a more empowering thought.

Examples are: I'll be okay. I'll figure it out. I'll always have enough. I am always safe. The people who love me for me will support me unconditionally. Other people may judge me, but what's more important is what I think of myself, and living a life that's true to me.

Now it's your turn.

_____

_____

_____

_____

_____

_____

_____

_____

_____

_____

_____

_____

_____

_____

_____

_____

_____

_____

_____
_____
_____
_____
_____
_____
_____
_____
_____
_____
_____
_____
_____
_____
_____
_____
_____
_____
_____
_____
_____
_____
_____
_____
_____
_____
_____
_____
_____

# Day 7: What no longer fills you up?

Throughout life, we change and grow. Dreams that used to fuel us no longer suit our current interests, desires and needs.

Maybe you got what you wanted, but the reality isn't as beautiful as the idea, or you've changed and no longer want this thing. Creating our dreams grows and changes us, as it should, and sometimes what once lit you up no longer does.

It's natural for our lives, dreams and goals to change as we do and the world does. It's important to honor these feelings rather than throw good energy after bad, getting lost in any stories keeping you stuck in a situation that doesn't make you happy.

Often our intuition knows it's time to change long before our conscious self does. The more you listen to your heart and trust yourself, the more you stay on the leading edge of these changes rather than get stuck or caught off guard.

Perhaps on the way to realizing a goal, you lost your way. It's okay. We all do it. This is a safe space to admit that so you can find your way back home.

The world changes, and this naturally creates new problems, desires and opportunities. We live in a fast-moving time and as industries revolutionize (or collapse), new possibilities appear as old ones cease to exist. Our dreams naturally shift in response to the changing world.

This is how it's supposed to be. I believe the universe answers collective prayers by planting dreams in our hearts. We're meant to take action on these dreams because the universe helps others through us.

Other times life happens, requiring us to shift. Athletes get injured. Women find out they can't have kids. A sickness changes your body in unalterable ways. Life happens in ways other than you expect.

Trust that it's all happening on purpose and for the highest good. You can create a beautiful life wherever you are, no matter what. And the more quickly you lean into what appear to be undesirable circumstances, the faster you move beyond them.

Honoring your evolution is important, including the ways you've changed and the ways your life has changed. Maybe you once wanted to travel and now feel the strange urge to settle down. Honor that.

Create a life that fulfills you now, based on who you are rather than who you were, who you think you should be, or what you think life should be. It's safe to change.

This takes the pressure off making changes, too. It's not like what you say or do now has to be forever. We have seasons in our lives. Maybe you go through a season of rooting down and creating a beautiful home for yourself, but then go through a season of expansion and travel only to settle back down. Life is not linear!

When one dream dies, another one is automatically born. It's the universal law. But we need to let go of the old by being honest with ourselves about what's no longer working in order to receive the new dream.

Sometimes we need to dwell in the space between, a space of nothingness, for what can seem like a long time. It may feel scary to not know what's next, but trust that after winter must come spring. The more you open up to the process, the more quickly and easily you'll be guided through.

The only constant in life is change. When we hold on to what was, refusing to allow old things to die, we block the birth of what wants to be. This results in feeling stuck, stagnant, trapped or confused.

It's not that what was wasn't real. It had a time, and that time is gone. The wisdom and experience you gained through creating what was will continue on in whatever you decide will be. You're not starting from scratch. You're starting from experience.

So today, get honest about what you're ready to release. What in your life has died that you're still holding onto? What's no longer working or no longer feels good? That might include a whole something or simply part of the whole. Where are you struggling to make things fit based on outdated ideas of who you are, how the world works or what life is supposed to be?

What evolutions are you resisting? Sometimes it's not entirely about letting go, but rather bringing a fresh energy or perspective to familiar things. The key is to get honest with yourself about where you're forcing or pushing and where you're being called to create space.

From this place of awareness, listen to your heart and feel into what comes next. Don't feel pressured to answer all of these questions! Free write and see what comes up.

_____

_____

_____

_____

_____
_____
_____
_____
_____
_____
_____
_____
_____
_____
_____
_____
_____
_____
_____
_____
_____
_____
_____
_____
_____
_____
_____
_____
_____
_____
_____
_____
_____
_____
_____

# Week 2: Clarifying who you are and what you want

Knowing who you are and what you want are the most essential ingredients to creating a life as unique as you!

This week, you'll connect deep within your heart to create this clarity.

At the end, you will feel so connected to yourself and inspired that you can create anything you dream of.

# Day 8: What do you most value?

Knowing your values is about getting clear on what matters to you so you can make better choices, resulting in a more fulfilling life. This isn't about what's right or wrong, but rather what's important to you.

Knowing your values will help design your life on the macro level while also helping you make better day-to-day decisions.

Sometimes people get really intellectual about this. To keep it simple, another way to ask this question is — what's important to you?

Today, your first task is to write down everything that matters. This could be your health, your career, your relationships. It could be causes you're passionate about like the environment or equality or helping animals. It could be ways of being like compassionate, authentic or kind.

Remember to pick things that make you FEEL something rather than things you think you should pick. We all have things we believe in. When designing your life, it's important to be clear about who you are and what's right for you.

Next, as you go about your week, stay aware of how you're making choices based on these values.

For example, let's say you're tempted to work late and finish a project. But you also haven't exercised yet that day. By creating awareness around your choices, and making them based on your values rather than in-the-moment impulses that may or may not be in your best interest, you can continue creating momentum toward your goals.

The important thing is making decisions from a place of being rooted in who you are and what's important to you, rather than what's important to other people. This requires strength because sometimes honoring your values will require you to say no to others or take an unpopular stand.

Your values will drive more fundamental life choices, too. If your life feels off, chances are something isn't aligning with your core values.

Maybe you value freedom, but have created a life of rigidity without space for serendipity or adventure.

Perhaps valuing freedom or autonomy means you'd do better working for yourself, or you need to find another creative way to experience more freedom. Meanwhile those who value structure and stability may find an office environment better suits their needs.

Maybe you value luxury but have been telling yourself it's wasteful to buy expensive things. Surrounding yourself with beautiful things that expand you only elevates your experience of life and motivates you to achieve your goals! Stay aware of any limiting beliefs telling you that what you want is wrong or impossible. Write them down.

Exploring another layer, maybe you tell yourself that freedom looks a certain way or you find reasons why you can't have what you want. In these cases, open up to creative solutions of the highest good. How can you create an experience of freedom or adventure right here, right now?

Maybe that looks like creating more unscheduled space in your calendar. Maybe that looks like taking more trips.

And if, for example, you tell yourself you can't travel, play with that. "If I could travel, what would that look like?"

Maybe you receive an idea about how to save or create more money. Perhaps you think of an inspired solution for any concerns, like how to care for children or pets. Maybe you realize that actually, the only thing between you and your dream was the thought you couldn't.

Or maybe, upon further questioning, you realize that you don't actually, for example, want to live location free, but you do long for adventure or more cultural experiences. This understanding can help you easily incorporate those things into your life.

To unlock this last layer, as you tune into what's most important to you, ask yourself — "What does a life that includes this value look like?"

Examples of values include freedom, courage, authenticity, kindness, open-mindedness, honesty, loyalty, family, passion, independence, health, accomplishment, collaboration, growth, adventure, honesty, determination and flexibility.

Try not to get too intellectual about this. Tune into your heart and ask: What's important to me? Write at least 20 things, and then go back through the list to pick your top 5.

When you're done, compare your values to your life choices. Is there something really important to you that you're not doing?

What are one or two changes you feel called to make right now? Starting today. Dive in!

_____
_____
_____

_____
_____
_____
_____
_____
_____
_____
_____
_____
_____
_____
_____
_____
_____
_____
_____
_____
_____
_____
_____
_____
_____
_____
_____
_____
_____
_____
_____
_____
_____
_____
_____
_____

# Day 9: What makes you unique?

Discovering who we are has a lot to do with identifying what makes us unique. It's the specific combination of gifts, talents, insights and ways we enjoy interacting with the world.

It's also a je ne sais quoi — an indescribable essence of you that you can feel. When making decisions, I like to feel into them and see if they feel like me.

While many people have many things in common, you have a unique combination of abilities, beliefs, interests, ways of seeing the world, talents and overall energetic essence that's like an energetic fingerprint.

When you stay connected to this unique energetic essence, you show up in the world as authentically you.

This is how you're guided along your unique path: by connecting to the unique energetic essence of you and using your inner wisdom to follow your intuition's next steps. This is the wisdom of your soul speaking to you in action.

This is also why mentally figuring out your life doesn't work. You must be courageous enough to follow your energetic impulse.

As you can imagine, this transcends logic, but for today, let's get super clear in exactly who you are. As you do, pay attention to how the words feel in your body. This is the essence of you.

For example: I am sweet and sassy, quirky and deep. I love to write and read and learn and ask questions. I love creating things. I love trying new things. I love riffing on new ideas. I love traveling, but am also a crazy homebody.

I think what makes me truly unique is that I am so beyond soft and sensitive, but also insanely tough. I can handle anything.

I'm a little bit of a contrarian, and I love that. Things work best for me when I totally trust myself and follow my instincts. I know deep down I am here to do things differently, to carve my own path.

I am a traveler, an explorer, and that includes exploring inner worlds. I love magic, but because I'm a Capricorn, I also have a streak of establishment in me although I hate to admit it.

I hope this inspires you as you explore what makes you, you.

Today, simply write down everything you know about yourself. Don't worry if it makes sense, or how it will all come together.

Just write about who you are and notice how it all feels. Connecting to yourself in this way will help you know your soul, which will allow you to follow its impulse and create a life as unique as you are.

_____

_____

_____

_____

_____

_____

_____

_____

_____

_____

_____

# Day 10: How do you best engage with the world?

We all have natural ways of showing up in the world, whether you're a natural leader, listener, encourager, gatherer or entertainer.

Maybe you uplift others. Perhaps you're curious, always digging deeper.

Some people are creative and endlessly thinking of new ideas. Others love debating, discussing provocative ideas or stirring the pot by playing Devil's advocate.

Maybe you're a gatherer who loves to throw parties and build community. Perhaps you're a soft, gentle presence who makes people feel at peace.

Knowing how you engage with the world, both how you like to show up and how you naturally make others feel, is a big part of knowing who you are.

This will give you permission to be that person, to cherish that person, rather than wish you were someone else, or waste energy trying to be someone else.

Figuring out how you like to engage with the world is foundational to helping you thrive in relationships and your career. It's about knowing how you show up in a way that's authentically you so you can become who you're meant to be.

This question will help you deepen into articulating your unique energetic essence that you began exploring yesterday. It's not necessary to get super analytical. This is more a process of tuning in and creating awareness. Your heart knows who you are even if you feel like you've forgotten.

Keep in mind that sometimes we do things that don't feel natural to gain new skills and grow. Every expert started out as a beginner. Just because you're not a natural at something doesn't mean you shouldn't do it. If you have a curiosity about something, by all means follow it!

Take a public speaking course if you're an introvert and feel called to do it. Take a cooking class even if you burn toast! This isn't about boxing yourself in, but giving yourself the freedom to experiment even if you discover it's not for you.

However, it's important to avoid losing what's authentically you as you discover new talents and try new things. Sometimes people feel that in order to become successful, find love or create a community, they need to change something about who they are.

You will need to try new things to create new things, yes, but you don't need to change who you fundamentally are. You are wonderful, worthy and whole right now. Create your life from a place of embracing who you are rather than feeling like you need to be a pretzel, bending yourself in various shapes to achieve your goals. That's how you lose yourself along the way.

Digging into this layer, take time to separate how you truly like to show up versus what you think is necessary or expected. Do you want a promotion but feel like you need a bigger personality to get it?

Or maybe you're a big personality who uplifts others but have always been told you're too much, and worry you're not serious enough even though you kick ass at your job.

It's time to own who you are and realize these fears come from others' judgments that you've taken on as your own. These judgments have nothing to do with you, but are projections of others' insecurities. This is an opportunity to see where you're judging yourself, which opens the way for greater self-acceptance.

Ultimately, this is about knowing the difference between how your heart feels called to evolve versus what you think you must do to be good enough to get what you want.

Also keep in mind that even our best qualities have dark, or shadow, sides when taken in extreme. For example, people who identify as good listeners or empaths need to make sure they feel heard and supported in relationships. Those who love caring for others need to make sure they allow themselves to be cared for.

Sometimes the way we engage with the world comes from unhealed wounds. When out of balance, these qualities stop serving us. The key is knowing when something brings you joy versus when it creates suffering.

If something brings you joy, it's from your heart. And if it creates suffering, it comes from an unhealed wound. We can dig deeper in another Soul Scroll journal. For now, think about how you like to engage in the world that brings you joy.

What exchanges leave you feeling the most fulfilled, energized and the most like you? Where are you telling yourself you need to change or be different to get what you want? What do you need to know to shift out of that story? Explore below.

_____

_____

_____

_____

_____

_____

_____

_____

_____

_____

_____

_____

_____

_____

_____

_____

_____

_____

_____

_____

_____

_____

_____

_____

_____

_____

_____

_____

_____

_____

# Day 11: What kind of person do you want to be?

Today is about deciding who you want to be and creating a perception of self reflecting your hopes and dreams, who you really are, rather than your fears and insecurities. We get to decide who we want to be, what qualities we want to cultivate, and what kind of lives we want to live.

This is built on a framework of total self-acceptance. Balancing that, however, is the truth that if you want to create different things, you must do different things. And to do different things, you must think of yourself in different ways.

All outside changes start within by changing your thoughts and energy. The foundation of this is acceptance for what is, which is why we spent so much time to create that acceptance.

This isn't limited by ANYTHING from the past or even the present, or what has or hasn't happened in your family or community. Who you become is entirely up to you.

During Week 1, you investigated the downside of this self-perception, and how who you think you are can limit you. Today is about the upside, and allowing your self-perception to expand you.

Keep in mind this will change throughout your life. Definitions are by nature limits, and what expands you now might limit you later. Definitely stay aware, but for today, tune in and see how you want to see yourself, framed by who you want to become.

Creating a roadmap for the kind of person you want to be allows you to select thoughts to nurture and ideas to follow through with. It influences the habits you cultivate and how you spend your days, which becomes how you spend your life.

For example, maybe you want to be a strong, compassionate, and fierce business woman. Or perhaps you see yourself as a kind and generous person who loves to support others. Maybe you see yourself as an adventurer who loves taking risks and cultivating thrills in life. Then again, maybe you love creating a cozy home space or love to think of yourself as a free thinker.

Maybe you desire to cultivate a mix of these things! Today's prompt is designed to help you create a new self concept and initiate an expansion beyond all previous limitation.

After you dream, create a few affirmations to support this new perception of self. Make sure the affirmations are in the present tense. These can change, so no pressure!

Ideas include: "I am adventurous, kind and fierce." "I am committed, smart and brave." "I am creative." "I never give up."

Now it's your turn. Who do you want to be? How does this person describe herself?

Notice any limiting thoughts that come up, especially around telling yourself "one day," or that you "aspire," to be or do something. Shifting your language into the present tense creates change now.

The truth is, you are these things now, even if they haven't happened yet! It's all a seed inside of you. Thinking of something as happening one day may indicate deeper fears around whether something is possible for you.

Think of the difference between, "One day I want to write a book," and, "I am writing a book." Thinking and speaking in the present tense inspires immediate action. Meanwhile, thinking "one day" creates space for procrastination and fear.

If a thought feels limiting or constrictive, ask for help from your inner guidance to see beyond it. Limiting thoughts aren't true! What do you *want* to believe?

We've honored your fears. Now it's time to honor your possibility.

_____

_____

_____

_____

_____

_____

_____

_____

_____

_____

_____

_____

_____

_____

_____

_____

_____

_____

_____
_____
_____
_____
_____
_____
_____
_____
_____
_____
_____
_____
_____
_____
_____
_____
_____
_____
_____
_____
_____
_____
_____
_____
_____
_____

# Day 12: What kind of life do you want to have lived?

One of the most powerful ways to ensure you do in life what matters is to stay connected to your mortality.

What do you want to have experienced or created? What do you want to be remembered for, even if only in your immediate circle? How do you want to make others feel? What would people say at your funeral?

This question might seem a little morbid, but something many accomplished people have in common is they frequently meditate on death.

Remembering the truth that we're all going to die puts things in perspective. Knowing your time is limited helps you overcome fears you may have of following your dreams.

You have one life. Will you spend it living someone else's? It's easy to do that when getting wrapped up in mundane things that don't really matter, forgetting your mortality.

Don't wait until a health scare before realizing that you never know how much time you have. It's easy to sacrifice your desires to meet responsibilities not realizing that if you die, the world will go on without you. It's a balance of course, but most people delay their dreams, never living them out. Don't let that happen to you.

You can only live life out of alignment with your true self for so long before emotional pain manifests as illness or disease. Maybe that sounds dramatic, but that's what happens!

Remembering your mortality helps you simultaneously take things less seriously as you think of things within the framework of a lifetime — will it matter in five months? — and take things more seriously as you understand there truly is no time to waste.

Time is the only non-renewable resource we have. You have to be smart with how you spend it.

We all have to face our deaths alone. Might as well learn how to be courageous now. Make sure you live how you want to have lived.

When you die, life will go on without you. The things you did for others because you convinced yourself they couldn't handle it alone — they'd figure it out.

But at the same time, maybe that inspires you to take an extra moment and be more kind. Smile at someone. Help someone even if you're busy. Shift your priorities. (We'll talk more about that later.)

For today — What kind of life do you want to live? What do you want to create or experience? What do you want your impact to be? How do you want to be remembered? There is no right or wrong. Listen to your heart.

_____
_____
_____
_____
_____
_____
_____
_____
_____

---
---
---
---
---
---
---
---
---
---
---
---
---
---
---
---
---
---
---
---
---
---
---
---
---
---
---
---
---
---
---
---
---
---
---
---

# Day 13: What do you most desire?

Today's question is simple and intentionally so. I'd love for you to free write about what you want — whatever comes up.

Nothing is off limits, too big, too much, too superficial, too unrealistic or too selfish. That's because you are not too big, too much, too superficial, too unrealistic or too selfish.

You are meant to want what you want. Your desires are sacred.

One of the reasons most people don't realize their desires is simply because they don't have clarity around what they are.

It can feel scary to admit what you want. We all have limiting beliefs that what we want isn't possible, or underlying fears of failure or loss or required sacrifice that stop us from taking action.

Women especially have unhealed trauma, individually, collectively and inherited from our family lines, that causes us to feel unsafe or unworthy when it comes to owning our desires, living boldly, and speaking our minds. You may feel guilty for wanting more, like you're doing something wrong, or anxious about admitting what you want.

Society STILL tends to tear down successful, opinionated, sexy women who fully own their power. People tell strong women to shut up, sit down, apologize for their views and put some clothes on. We're taught to apologize for our bodies, our opinions, our needs, desires and our very being.

It's time for us to face these demons within ourselves and applaud fully expressed women while creating space for ourselves to become fully self-expressed. Other people's opinions have nothing to do with your life.

Stay aware of any physical sensations or thoughts this exercise evokes within you. Be present with them but don't let them stop you. It's time to break free. You are strong enough to handle whatever comes your way. It's worth it to live the life of your dreams.

A lot of times it feels scary to name our desires because it involves choice. It's natural to worry about choosing the right thing. Know there is no right or wrong in the game of life! Everything is either a lesson or a blessing. Everything is helping you become who you're meant to be, if you believe it is.

You can always change your mind, but deciding is very important. Without deciding your desires, you will lack clarity and drift along. You'll feel a sense of waiting. Whatever you're waiting for isn't coming because the thing you are waiting for is you! Your own decision, clarity and commitment.

In the absence of decision, you won't make meaningful progress in your life. This creates a sense of powerlessness and stagnation.

You'll spend time focusing on your problems or other people's lives, especially on social media. You could feel frustrated, like there's no room for you, or like you're living somebody else's life.

You may even blame outside people or circumstances, but it all began because you lacked a clear vision for where you're going, or didn't choose the courage to create it.

This is how people get stuck. We get too focused on our problems or past and not focused enough on a vision of what we're creating. The good news is you can shift out of neutral and into drive any time.

So today, decide. Get clear on what you want. Allow yourself to receive the vision of your heart. Notice the doubts and fears, but decide to no longer let them control you. This is a time to hear your heart without judgment or censorship.

It can help to meditate first and really connect in. Head to SoulScrollJournals.com/bonuses for a free guided meditation to help you do just that.

Know that the universe placed these desires in your heart because the infinite intelligence wants you to live them out. Your desires are intended to pull you forward into the person you want to become.

You were born to be powerful, creative and strong. A force of good in the world.

Again, there is no right or wrong. Your desires are part of the unfolding of the ever-changing universe, no matter how small or large. Following the calling of your heart is what allows the infinite creative potential of the universe to flow through you and use your life for good. As you expand, the universe expands because you are part of it and it is part of you.

So today, go within and listen to your heart. Give voice to what you truly, deeply want. If at any time, a voice says, "But I don't know," ask, "If I did know, what would I want?" You might also ask, "Why am I afraid to admit what I want?"

And then end with the original question — What do you most desire?

_____

_____

# Day 14: What would feel really fun and exciting to add into your life right now?

We've cleared a lot of space over the last week! You now know yourself in a much deeper way. Go you!

Yesterday's question was very big picture. Today is all about zooming into the present and connecting to your next right step.

By now, you're tuned into your values. You know what kind of a world you believe in. You understand who you want to be and what you really want.

All these things lie inside of you. New parts of your subconscious are activated. They will influence you no matter what.

Don't worry about trying to figure out how to to make it all come together or how to achieve your big-picture vision. Don't analyze what to do next from some heavy feeling there's a right or wrong thing to do.

Instead, allow the energy of the work you've done to uplift and fulfill you. From this energetic place of connection to yourself, simply ask — what would feel fun and exciting to add into my life right now?

It might be something small. You might feel inspired to start a new fitness habit, organize your house or cook healthier, more fun meals.

You might have the idea to start a new creative project, to paint or take a class. If you're having trouble deciding between a few ideas, what feels the most energizing or exciting?

Even if you're worried about figuring out your career or finding your purpose, I guarantee the way to find the answers is to follow your heart forward, one next right step at a time.

The truth about figuring out your life is there's never anything to figure out. It's simply about connecting to yourself, knowing who you are, setting the intention for what you want to create and trusting your inner guidance as it leads you forward — even if the guidance feels totally random or unrelated. Trust it's all part of the process.

All this inner work is like setting a destination into Google maps. You don't have to know HOW it will all come together, only trust that it will. In fact, there's no way to know how.

How could you know how to do something you've never done? You have no choice but to follow your intuition because your inner being is the only one with directions for manifesting your desires.

You'll create your beautiful life one next right step at a time, guided by the deeper vision and values you're now connected to.

We're taught to plan, strategize and over-schedule our lives, but our true power and intelligence doesn't lie in the conscious mind. It lies in the connection to your heart, in the universe, and in your subconscious mind, which is one with the universal intelligence, the source of all that is.

This way of living makes life a fun adventure. The more you trust yourself and follow the flow, the more you'll see how the universe delivers magical synchronicities to help you co-create a life beyond your wildest dreams. Tuning into your heart is how you receive the unexpected insights required to achieve your goals.

Thinking too much limits your possibilities. The mind only knows what it's experienced. Living from the mind causes us to re-create the past. To create something new, we have to follow our hearts. Embrace not knowing and uncertainty. Trust yourself to move forward into the unknown as you follow your intuition.

Another note: It's easy to get over-inspired and try to do a million things at once. If you feel called, definitely do. However in my experience, it helps to focus on one or two new projects or goals at a time. Focus makes it easier to build positive momentum. It's important to do something long enough to fully decide if it's right for you. This isn't about the energy of dabbling, but the energy of commitment to creating something new.

So today ask: What feels fun to add into your life right now? What's your next right step? And then take action!

_____

_____

_____

_____

_____

_____

_____

_____

_____

_____

_____

---------------------------------------------------

---------------------------------------------------

---------------------------------------------------

---------------------------------------------------

---------------------------------------------------

---------------------------------------------------

---------------------------------------------------

---------------------------------------------------

---------------------------------------------------

---------------------------------------------------

---------------------------------------------------

---------------------------------------------------

---------------------------------------------------

---------------------------------------------------

---------------------------------------------------

---------------------------------------------------

---------------------------------------------------

---------------------------------------------------

---------------------------------------------------

---------------------------------------------------

---------------------------------------------------

---------------------------------------------------

---------------------------------------------------

---------------------------------------------------

# Week 3: Designing your next level

It's time to tune into the person you are becoming and discover how to create that transformation right now!

This week is going to be super fun.

# Day 15: What do you need to feel nourished, alive and radiant?

A lot of times people find themselves feeling stuck or unhappy when they've put themselves last for a long time, forgetting to fill their lives with the things that bring them joy. Forgetting to nourish themselves mind, body and spirit.

It's not selfish to take time / ask for help to create the time / say no or set boundaries so you have time for you. It's selfish not to.

And it does no good to sacrifice your wellbeing while pursuing external goals because if you lose your wellbeing in the process, you won't have the energy to achieve your goals or enjoy life!

Running yourself ragged creates unhappiness and resentment. It causes you to (dis)engage in life from a place of depletion and exhaustion. Lacking life-force energy, your actions create weak results, perhaps creating a toxic cycle where you work even harder rather than release and rest.

In these times, you may find yourself feeling sad, defeated or critical. You may feel like everything's a struggle and wonder what you're doing wrong. You may blame yourself or outside circumstances when the deeper truth is that you put yourself last, and so life put you last.

Taking time to meditate and exercise, daydream, walk in the park or watch movies, paint or pursue creative projects that bring you joy will nourish your spirit, reigniting your joie de vivre.

As you interact with life from a place of being lit from within, you'll find external circumstances shifting as they magically begin to work in your favor.

This is the essence of creating an extraordinary life, one that's as unique as you are. It's also part of manifesting. As you connect to the joy within, you will magnetize new circumstances reflecting this uplifted internal state.

If you feel stuck in life, increasing your self-care is an often-overlooked key that unlocks the flow of fun and abundance.

Taking time to care for yourself with healthy food, exercise, rest and relaxation isn't optional. It's the equivalent of filling your car with gas so you can get back on the road.

Tank full, you'll feel better. This allows you to enjoy the journey and stop obsessing over the destination.

Living this way gives you a stronger connection to your inner guidance. And the actions you do take will be more effective simply because you're infusing them with more of your precious life-force energy.

So take some time now and connect to the energy or vision of your future self, the person you want to become.

How does she care for herself? What makes you feel joyful, energized or radiant? If you're not sure, what do you think might help you feel that way? Again, there is no right or wrong, only however you feel called to care for yourself.

As a quick note, it can be fun to dream big with this. Maybe your future self receives weekly massages or hires someone to clean her house, but that's not in your current budget.

How can you move toward this goal? Maybe you get a massage monthly or every other month right now, or re-allocate some of your budget to a cleaning person, giving you more time to work towards your dreams. Simply set the intention and allow your desires to inspire your way forward.

After journaling, create an action plan and do it!

_____

_____

_____

_____

_____

_____

_____

_____

_____

_____

_____

_____

_____

_____

_____

_____

_____

_____

_____

_____

---

---

---

---

---

---

---

---

---

---

---

---

---

---

---

---

---

---

---

---

---

---

---

---

---

---

---

---

---

---

---

---

---

# Day 16: What are your priorities in life?

Today, let's get clear on your priorities so you have time for everything that matters. Earlier you explored your values, so you're connected to what's important to you. Today is about identifying what is MOST important to you.

Keep in mind this will fluctuate, but knowing your baseline will help you make better choices.

This may challenge some of the roles you play, as identified during Week 1. Stay conscious of this as you dive in. As a benefit of this exercise, you'll make decisions that nurture you. Let's say caring for yourself and others both matter to you. However right now, without clear priorities, you may have few boundaries or none at all, which zaps your energy, depletes your time, and fills you with resentment.

Consider how life will look if you choose to prioritize yourself. You can, in the moment, recognize when you're feeling depleted and know that saying yes to a request would violate your priority of caring for yourself.

Or, maybe prioritizing yourself has paid off, giving you abundant energy and a sincere desire to offer care. Then saying yes is totally in integrity. You'll help from joy rather than obligation. (And feel less selfish for saying "no" later on!)

This is the key to shifting out of autopilot. Instead, you're empowered, shifting gears in every moment, adjusting as needed to whatever life throws your way. You're fully rooted in who you are, what you need, and what matters to you — and in what order.

No longer are you controlled by guilt and shoulds, and even if you feel guilty, you know that you ARE the kind of person who helps others — when you have the capacity.

This is also about recognizing that if you have creative dreams, such as writing a book, starting a business or learning a new skill, you've got to prioritize them even if that requires shifting expectations or asking for help in other areas of your life. Otherwise your dreams won't happen.

Achieving your dreams doesn't require many hours each day, but rather a commitment to devoting some time consistently. Write 500 words a day and in 3 or 4 months, you'll be an actual author. Spend 30 minutes a day painting, and your masterpiece will be done in record time.

This work sets the foundation to create a life as unique as you.

Let's dive in:

Step 1: Write down everything that matters to you. Arrange this list in numerical order of priority.

These choices will feel hard. That's okay. They won't be cut-and-dry. Your choices will be fluid because life is. But it's important to know what matters, and in what order so you can consciously design your life.

Step 2: Identify what people, places and activities in your life deplete you, feel like a should or a burden, or are total wastes of time. Maybe your heart keeps telling you to stop some things, but you continue anyway.

Ask: Do you really have to do these things? Why do you do them?

If you don't need these things, cross them off your list. If you do, how can you reframe to acknowledge that spending this energy is a conscious choice? (It always is.) How can you eliminate, reduce or shift those things that feel heavy? Feel free to ask the universe for a creative solution of the highest good.

Step 3: How do you wish to fill the space you've created? Maybe you want to scroll your phone less and read more. (Or scroll your soul!) Simply setting an intention here is powerful and will help you create change over time.

If you need to go deeper, explore any conflicts you're experiencing. Work and family, for instance, likely both matter. Which do you prioritize? How can you integrate the two? How can you allot energy to each in a way that honors what's true for you?

This is less about making hard-and-fast rules and more about learning to tune in and see what you need in each moment, with established priorities as a foundational guide. This is also about becoming sovereign in your life, making your own decisions rather than living by external expectation.

This is a lifelong journey and not something to figure out today. It's also a big topic. Depending on whether you've done exercises like this before, maybe dip a toe in. If this is something you've visited before, dive deeper.

Either way, you can always return later. Do what you can!

_____

_____

_____
_____
_____
_____
_____
_____
_____
_____
_____
_____
_____
_____
_____
_____
_____
_____
_____
_____
_____
_____
_____
_____
_____
_____
_____
_____
_____
_____
_____
_____

# Day 17: What does the absolute best version of your life right now look like?

Sometimes dreams feel far away and it's easy to think that because of where you are, you can't get where you want to be.

If that's the case, take heart: you have everything you need to take the next right step in the direction of your dreams.

We always have more opportunities than we can see. The problem is we're biologically wired to focus on potential dangers and threats, which is a survival instinct. This was great when we needed to outrun grizzly bears to survive, but it doesn't help us thrive.

When you're focused on staying safe or looking for what's wrong, you miss what's going right. You miss the opportunities in front of you, those that come into view once you let down your guard, stop planning for worst-case scenarios and wide your gaze.

If you've been feeling stuck, know that something as simple as beginning a new project, starting an exercise routine or learning a new hobby can be the key to re-energizing your life.

Realizing your dreams is all about taking one right next step at a time. Doing what you can, with what you have, where you are, and wisely using all the resources available to you right now. As you intentionally use all your existing resources, you will receive more.

For those chasing big dreams: While it's important to dream big and set invigorating goals, sometimes we set goals so huge it seems like we can't achieve them no matter how hard we try. This can create suffering too, if we end up focusing on the future and ignoring the present.

If you've been feeling stuck in place for a while, connect with your goals. Are they really your goals, or things you think will make you good enough? If they are your goals, is it a Chapter 10 goal while you're on Chapter 2? If you had a right-next-step or incremental goal, what would that be?

Something else to think about is creating balance by setting goals in multiple areas of life. When you're really focused on growth in a specific area of life, it's easy to obsess. Deficiencies in other areas of our lives result. Energetic imbalance will eventually create physical imbalance. That's why inner harmony and a vision for all areas of your life is essential.

If you'd like support around this, check out the Play with the Day yearly goal journal, which guides you through the process of setting a vision in all areas of your life. It also supports you with monthly intention and goal setting and daily habit tracking.

Balance looks different for every person, every day and in every season of life, but nourishing all aspects of our lives in some way is essential. This is what creates joy. It's also what allows us to expand from a sense of being grounded in the moment, in our lives, and in ourselves. This is how to create sustainable growth.

Creating an extraordinary life is about thinking big, with your eyes toward the sky but your feet on the ground. Expanding so fully and joyfully into the present moment that your life has no choice but to expand around you.

This allows you to grow through joy rather than force. This way prepares your nervous system and energy fields to receive increasingly greater amounts of love, joy, success and prosperity.

Today, reconnect and look at your life with the perspective of an outsider or friend. If you were giving yourself advice on how to best live your life right now, what would you say?

What would you do differently? What would you be more grateful for? What opportunities would you take advantage of? What would you no longer tolerate? What bad habits would you let go of? In what ways would your goals change, if at all?

How can you more fully expand into all the resources and opportunities available to you, in a way that feels aligned and soulful and exciting?

Let your soul speak!

_____

_____

_____

_____

_____

_____

_____

_____

_____

_____

_____

_____

_____

_____

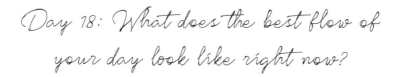

*Day 18: What does the best flow of your day look like right now?*

A common personal development exercise is to write about your perfect average day in an ideal life. Today you'll explore the Soul Scroll Journals' spin on this exercise by identifying the best flow for your day in your life right now.

Focusing too much on an ideal that will never exist can cause a dissonance creating suffering and resistance. Resistance doesn't motivate you to create meaningful change, but instead keeps you focused on what you don't have, consequently continuing to create a life that doesn't make you happy.

Life is right here, right now. When you create joy and happiness in the present moment, you expand into it. The more you expand into the present moment, creating a string of joyful todays, the more easily and effortlessly you expand toward your dreams.

But rather than feeling stressed the whole time, or like you were never doing enough or as if you should be further along than you are, you'll have enjoyed the whole ride.

You'll have created a life that's uniquely you rather than something you thought you wanted but that actually doesn't bring you much joy even if it looks perfect on the outside.

The power in this exercise is that it helps you identify simple changes you can make right now to add more joy and meaning to your life. You may identify a lot of potential changes. Don't let that overwhelm you! Take one step at a time.

I encourage you to, after finishing the exercise, connect to one or two small, specific shifts you want to make right now.

If you'd like to start new habits, check out Soul Scroll Journals' Play with the Day yearly goal journal. It has space for monthly goals and intentions, along with a habit tracker to support your journey of making incremental shifts that add up for lasting change.

Now then, onto today's exercise. Questions to consider:

What do you do first thing in the morning? Do you have a morning ritual. If so, what does it look like? What time do you wake up? How do you feel after waking up?

What kind of clothes do you wear? How do you prepare yourself for the day?

When do you work, if you work? What do you work on? What kinds of projects do you do? How does your working space feel? How do your working relationships feel? What is your relationship to work?

What do you do in the afternoon or after work?

What do you eat? Where do you eat, and with whom? Do you have any meal systems, like meal prep or someone to help you with food or even food delivery?

How do you move your body? What type of exercise do you do and when?

What about in the evenings? How do you wind down for bed? Do you have a ritual you like to follow? If so, what is it?

How do you feel at the end of the day? What do you tell yourself?

The overall structure of your day is very important. While nobody likes being stuck in a routine that feels boring or uninspiring, finding a basic flow that provides you with a level of consistency and includes time for everything that's important to you is key for creative fulfillment, success, joy and an overall sense of peacefulness.

We all usually do the same things every day anyway. This is an opportunity to become conscious of how you're using your time and tweak the life you have right now so it brings you joy.

Feeling joyful in the present moment is a clear indication you're headed in the right direction. Follow your joy. It will show you exactly how to design a life of meaning and purpose, step by step, feeling good right now rather than obsessing over an imagined ideal that, the more you obsess over it, seems to run further away.

_____

_____

_____

_____

_____

_____

_____

_____

_____

_____

_____

_____

_____

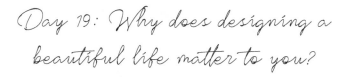

*Day 19: Why does designing a beautiful life matter to you?*

Creating real, sustainable change requires a deep why. It's awesome to want material things including money and travel and nice clothes and cars and other fancy things.

But what really drives us, and what will give you the fuel to keep going amid any setbacks or feelings of failure, is a deep why.

And this IS deep. I once saw someone post online that her why was because she wanted to go on Target shopping sprees.

There's nothing wrong with that desire, but a powerful why is something that when you think about it, makes you want to cry. It moves you. It motivates you and inspires you when you feel like giving up.

It can be nice to connect to two different whys: A why for you and a why for the world.

Personally, when I feel like giving up and feel like nobody cares what I'm doing, a why for the world doesn't motivate me. I need to connect back to what creating the life of my dreams means to ME.

But having a why for the world is also important because it connects everything back to service, to helping create the kind of world you believe in. This helps you feel connected to something bigger than you, which contributes to a sense of meaning and fulfillment.

Feeling connected to these two whys injects your work and life with a sense of purpose and importance. A caveat: This can change.

Don't let it turn into something that ends up holding you hostage.

Your personal why might relate to deeper values like freedom, including time and financial freedom. A why for the world might might relate to the kind of world you believe in, a specific way you want to see the world change or a cause you're passionate about. It might be about how you know your work impacts others.

Either one might be a personal mission, to show yourself what's possible, or to create a better life for your children.

There is no right or wrong here, but it is good to go as deep as possible. Just keep asking yourself — why? Why do you want the things you do? And when you connect to that, ask again. But why?

Keep asking again and again until you hit something that gives you goosebumps, brings you to tears, or unlocks a deep connection to the core of you. Your why.

You might want to write this down or revisit it in some way every day. This is what will motivate you and direct everything you do.

---------------------------------------------------------------

---------------------------------------------------------------

---------------------------------------------------------------

---------------------------------------------------------------

---------------------------------------------------------------

---------------------------------------------------------------

---------------------------------------------------------------

---------------------------------------------------------------

---------------------------------------------------------------

_____
_____
_____
_____
_____
_____
_____
_____
_____
_____
_____
_____
_____
_____
_____
_____
_____
_____
_____
_____
_____
_____
_____
_____
_____
_____
_____
_____
_____
_____

# Day 20: What beliefs don't align with where you're going?

By now you're connected to what you want, what's important to you, and why it matters. You're connected to where you want to go.

What fears or doubts have come up as you've identified your dreams and bigger vision? Do you feel like you could never be that successful, make that kind of money, have that kind of impact, live that kind of life?

Do you beat yourself up when you make mistakes, which stops you from trying new things? Do you get overwhelmed and quit when you feel unsure rather than commit to continually showing up, trusting that your skills will improve and that you will get better?

Does the fear of others' judgment paralyze you, stopping you from doing what you want to do? Do you tell yourself you don't have time, or that it's not the right time, to follow your dreams?

Today is an opportunity to get honest about what fears or negative thoughts are keeping you from creating your dreams. Write them down and ask — where did they come from? How can you see them differently? What new story would you like to tell yourself about who you are and what's possible for you?

Create an affirmation you can remind yourself of whenever old, negative thoughts come up.

To shift, I find it helpful to work through my thoughts and feelings to shift to a new story. This helps because fighting your thoughts creates resistance which only magnifies what you're trying to avoid. Negative thoughts are only evidence of fear or unhealed past pains. Honoring the fear or any pain that arises helps dissolve it.

Here's sample self-talk you can use: "I know that sometimes you feel afraid that what you want isn't possible, or you could never have a life like that. I understand it feels scary to make changes. But I really believe in you, and I have faith that by taking one next right step at a time, we can create really cool things in this life."

Another good affirmation is, "Even though I feel afraid, I love myself deeply and completely."

As you create new neural pathways, shifting to more positive thoughts will become easier. At first, it might feel hard. You may have a lot of painful emotions built up enforcing the negative beliefs. Feel any feelings that rise up by simply becoming aware of them and breathing into the sensations. The meditation on SoulScrollJournals.com/bonuses guides you through this process.

This practice releases the stuck emotions attached to any fear-based beliefs. As you release the underlying emotional energy, you create space to believe new, more positive thoughts.

The key to working with your thoughts is staying aware of what you actually believe versus what makes you feel doubt underneath. If you feel an affirmation as solidly true, then go for it. But if you feel doubt, fear or pain underneath of it, spend time feeling your feelings, understanding your fear and working through the related thoughts.

You can also create a transitional affirmation, and say something like, "I want to believe...," or, "I am learning to believe..."

Reprograming your mind and healing your heart this way takes time. You've been creating these negative neural grooves for decades, and it takes awareness and time to create new, more positive pathways.

Committing to telling a new story for as long as it takes is key. This process can take a lot of emotional energy. Some days it will feel like you're not getting anywhere although truly, each shift makes a big difference! Stay with it.

Humans repeat the same few thoughts over and over again throughout the day. You have two choices: Continue to repeat thoughts that keep you trapped and stuck you or commit to the process of reprogramming your mind so you can create a life you love.

Don't give up. Keep repeating the new, more positive thoughts until they become embedded in your subconscious and become part of who you are. But also — and this is very important — create space to be with your heart and feel any feelings that come up to release them. As you create peace within, believing these new, more empowering thoughts will be easy.

Sometimes it's enough to simply feel and release the emotion. You don't always have to consciously understand what exactly you're releasing. Have faith! You are moving mountains.

_____

_____

_____
_____
_____
_____
_____
_____
_____
_____
_____
_____
_____
_____
_____
_____
_____
_____
_____
_____
_____
_____
_____
_____
_____
_____
_____
_____
_____
_____
_____

_____
_____
_____
_____
_____
_____
_____
_____
_____
_____
_____
_____
_____
_____
_____
_____
_____
_____
_____
_____
_____
_____
_____
_____
_____
_____
_____
_____

# Day 21: Connect to your future self and receive a message from her.

We always have access to our past and future selves. Any time you feel afraid and unsure, you can tap into your future self and receive guidance or support from her.

No matter what's happening in your life, there's always a version of you who is grounded and confident, assured and strong. She is happy and successful, and has created everything that today's version of you dreams about.

Tune into this future version of you. How does she stand? What is she doing? What is she wearing? What does she look like? What does she want to tell you?

Every time you need to make a decision, whether what to eat for lunch or what project to work on next, you can tune into the future you and receive her guidance.

What would the you who has already created your desired reality do?

What decision most aligns with your goals, values and priorities, with who you really are? You know the way by how it feels.

Those times you make decisions that don't feel good, it's nothing to beat yourself up about. Simply become aware and choose again. Love yourself. You are learning. You are in process. That's how it's supposed to be. Everything is perfect exactly as it is.

You will get where you want to go, and you're exactly where you're meant to be.

The you right now is amazing. You are perfect as you are and beyond enough and worthy of love. But because you're here, I know you want more. You know there's more inside of you. It's time to create that! Connecting to your future self can show you how.

Another thing to try is to keep this image in your mind. The mental images we hold convey a lot of power. They imprint our subconscious minds, which drive our decision making.

Become aware of the mental images you're holding and make sure they reflect your desires and not your fears!

Know that your subconscious mind is connected to the universal mind, the infinite source. As you impress images into your subconscious mind, you are creating that reality and drawing the resources and people reflecting those images toward you.

This is the essence of quantum creation, and exactly why holding images of happiness and abundance, health and prosperity is so important.

Every day you make a choice — which version of the future you are you moving toward? What kind of images are you holding in your mind?

On that note, tune into the future version of you and ask what message she has for you today.

_____
_____
_____
_____
_____
_____

---

# Week 4: Becoming limitless

This week you'll taste the exhilaration of limitlessness. No matter what the past has held, you can create anything you want to.

Get ready to prepare your mind and heart to step into your extraordinary life.

# Day 22: How capable do you feel of success?

Underneath a lot of stalled dreams are fears that you don't have what it takes to succeed, fears of failure and judgment, fears that because of where you are, you can't get where you want to be.

Often we believe limiting ideas about our abilities or talents or capacity to achieve based on things other people have told us throughout our lives.

Maybe your parents or a teacher spoke discouraging words over you, proclaiming you'd never amount to anything or weren't smart.

Maybe someone told you in words or action that your natural talents weren't good enough or they could never make you money, or that a sibling was more talented than you.

Maybe you've tried to follow your dreams but experienced disappointment or failure you haven't recovered from. Today is a time to see things differently. It's time to heal.

It's time to become full of yourself, which I consider to mean full of your own spirit, overflowing with radiance. You are beyond capable and worthy of creating whatever you desire.

It doesn't matter what disappointments or failures or cruel words the past has held for you. The future becomes bright the moment you let your connection to your inner light become the truth.

No matter where you are right now, you can always get where you want to be.

Today, ask yourself what you believe about your talents or ability to succeed. Get clear on all the false ideas that could hold you back. Shine the light of awareness into all the dark places.

In doing so, know that you are removing the power from that pain. It will no longer control you. You are good enough. You are worthy and talented. Your future is bright. The world needs the unique gifts, insights and energy you have to offer.

After creating awareness, journal about what you'd rather believe about success or your ability to realize your dreams. Tune into your higher self, your heart, the future version of you or the universe for guidance if you feel called.

Example beliefs include, "I can achieve anything I put my mind to. I am good at what I do. I deserve success and abundance. I'm smart and capable. I am resourceful, always able to figure things out. What is right for me will not pass me by. Everything is always working out for me. I may have experienced failure, but I am not a failure. Believing in possibility makes everything possible."

Tune into your heart and your soul. Write whatever comes up!

---------------------------------------------------------------

---------------------------------------------------------------

---------------------------------------------------------------

---------------------------------------------------------------

---------------------------------------------------------------

---------------------------------------------------------------

---------------------------------------------------------------

---------------------------------------------------------------

---
---
---
---
---
---
---
---
---
---
---
---
---
---
---
---
---
---
---
---
---
---
---
---
---
---
---
---
---
---
---
---
---

# Day 23: Why do you NOT want your dreams to come true?

Underneath a lot of blocks, stuck feelings or inabilities to create the success you want are deeper fears about what would happen if you got everything you wanted.

This might seem weird — like, of course I want the things I want! But often our deepest desires conflict with deeper fears about costs we may not be willing to pay.

These fears may or may not be true, but they'll control you unless you become aware of them.

For example, maybe you're afraid that succeeding will come at a high cost, like sacrificing your health or family time or happiness. Maybe you or your parents believed that, and consequently created that reality in the past. Know that you can create a new reality where you get to succeed while following your truest dreams AND radiate health and happiness. You get to be rich AND have rewarding relationships. You get to have it all!

Maybe you're afraid that getting what you want would make you too powerful or confident, and worry deep down that those you love won't love you anymore if you become that person.

Perhaps a parent or other beloved figure in your life wanted certain things from you, or even actively opposes your dreams and desires, and you're worried this person would no longer love you if you followed your heart. Maybe you've come to terms with your parents not supporting you, but now subconsciously fear your partner won't support you or that your kids would resent you.

We all dream of realizing our deepest desires, but subconscious fears of how that would impact your everyday life may squash that vision before it has a chance to grown. Sometimes these deeper fears are the entire reason we buy into more surface-level fears of not having the money, time or talent.

Speaking of money: Maybe you're afraid that following your heart would require you to be broke (you can make money doing anything), or that if you did become wealthy, people would think of you as greedy or superficial.

These are just some of the inner fears we face that stop us from taking action on our dreams and finding fulfillment

These examples have likely stirred things up, so take a pen now and journal it out. Why do you not want your dreams to come true? What are you afraid would happen if you did get everything you wanted?

After getting these fears down on paper, ask your higher self for help seeing things differently.

What would you rather believe? What in your heart do you know to be true?

For example, those who truly love you will love you no matter what. And even if they don't, is that someone you want in your life? Are you willing to sacrifice an authentic, fulfilling life to appease someone whose love is false, and not real?

The likelihood, even if you fear otherwise, is that the people around you will understand. They want you to be happy.

Everything that's in your heart is ultimately for the highest good. That means it's good for you and for everyone around you.

The universe wouldn't give you a heartfelt desire if it was bad for the world.

Whatever you need help seeing differently, trust that your inner self has the guidance to help you with that realization.

---------------------------------------------------------------
---------------------------------------------------------------
---------------------------------------------------------------
---------------------------------------------------------------
---------------------------------------------------------------
---------------------------------------------------------------
---------------------------------------------------------------
---------------------------------------------------------------
---------------------------------------------------------------
---------------------------------------------------------------
---------------------------------------------------------------
---------------------------------------------------------------
---------------------------------------------------------------
---------------------------------------------------------------
---------------------------------------------------------------
---------------------------------------------------------------
---------------------------------------------------------------
---------------------------------------------------------------
---------------------------------------------------------------
---------------------------------------------------------------
---------------------------------------------------------------
---------------------------------------------------------------
---------------------------------------------------------------

---------------------------------------------------------------

---------------------------------------------------------------

---------------------------------------------------------------

---------------------------------------------------------------

---------------------------------------------------------------

---------------------------------------------------------------

---------------------------------------------------------------

---------------------------------------------------------------

---------------------------------------------------------------

---------------------------------------------------------------

---------------------------------------------------------------

---------------------------------------------------------------

---------------------------------------------------------------

---------------------------------------------------------------

---------------------------------------------------------------

---------------------------------------------------------------

---------------------------------------------------------------

---------------------------------------------------------------

---------------------------------------------------------------

---------------------------------------------------------------

---------------------------------------------------------------

---------------------------------------------------------------

---------------------------------------------------------------

---------------------------------------------------------------

---------------------------------------------------------------

# Day 24: In a world with no limits, what would you be / do / have?

Today is probably the funnest day! And no, funnest isn't a word, but today is all about dropping limitation, so what a perfect segue into our conversation.

Most people construct their lives based on ideas of how they think things should be, as we've been talking about. We tell ourselves stories about what we need to do "or else," we'll lose something sacred.

There are a few layers to this conversation. The first is removing the need to take the conventional path, like working the unfulfilling office job because people expect you to or it's what you studied, but it doesn't make you happy.

Perhaps you've heard this before, but still think: How else am I supposed to make money? Know that everything is ultimately a choice. Nobody is forcing you to do anything, and if you do feel forced, it might be good to examine that story! You can achieve any dream in your heart with enough creativity and courage.

The second layer will resonate with those already walking an unconventional path, but who feel unfulfilled. Ironically more people than ever before are stepping off the corporate ladder-climbing ideal, but now a conventional unconventional ideal has formed.

So many people are starting online businesses becoming life coaches or selling courses or becoming influencers or yoga teachers or living in vans while traveling the world.

Those things are all amazing — if it's what YOU want. It's easy to find ourselves inspired / manipulated by ideals on social media that don't actually exist. Do you want what you want because you want it, or because it looked cool on Instagram and you thought it would make you happy?

Does this dream fire you up and inspire you to take action? If not, maybe it's not your dream. Give yourself permission to ask: If not this, what else would I do?

Creating space for a new dream is necessary to receive it, even if creating that space feels scary. Dreams can't come to us if we crowd them out with limiting ideas about what's not possible or what we think is required of us. There's always an inspired solution of the highest good. Shift your focus from problems to possibilities, from obstacles to opportunities.

Your soul has unique gifts and a special way to give them. Trust that. The way to find the unique path you're meant to walk is by following your intuition one step at a time.

However, it's also important to set aside time to receive the larger vision for your life, and that's what we're doing today.

There's no right or wrong in this exercise, and there are no limits! Maybe the corporate life IS for you. Or maybe you ARE meant to become a life coach or sell online courses or be an influencer. But maybe you have an off-the-wall idea that's never been done before. Trust that.

Be careful to draw conclusions about money, too. Some people want the luxe life and others desire a simple one. Dropping out of convention doesn't necessarily mean making do with less money. Sometimes it does, or maybe at the beginning, but trust that if you have the desire to earn big AND follow your dreams, you can do both.

You don't have to choose. This is a world without limit! The only thing that matters is — does it make you happy?

Today, tune in, sit with yourself in silence and ask to be shown a vision. Write down what you see, as far as you can see, whether that's five feet in front of you or 5,000.

_____
_____
_____
_____
_____
_____
_____
_____
_____
_____
_____
_____
_____
_____
_____
_____
_____
_____
_____

_____
_____
_____
_____
_____
_____
_____
_____
_____
_____
_____
_____
_____
_____
_____
_____
_____
_____
_____
_____
_____
_____
_____
_____
_____
_____
_____

# Day 25: What thoughts and beliefs support your unlimited vision?

Today is a fun day, too! Yesterday you went deep into your biggest and highest vision for what you desire to create and experience in life. You might want to go back and read what you wrote.

Over the past few weeks, you've illuminated deeper fears along with existing thoughts and beliefs creating a story, a narrative of reality that upholds an experience of life that isn't taking you where you want to go.

You've also started creating new thoughts and beliefs, and therefore a new story, that will help you create the life you dream of.

Since thoughts are alive energy, thinking the thoughts aligned with what you want to create will connect you to the inspired guidance necessary to create it. It will also help you feel more confident and secure in yourself.

After clarifying the thoughts and beliefs you want to adopt, remind yourself of them all day long. It might be helpful to write your vision or a few affirmations down in your journal each morning.

As you go through your day, notice the thoughts you're thinking. When thoughts that don't feel good arise, simply notice them and remind yourself of what you'd rather believe. (Having a go-to affirmation, such as "I can achieve anything I put my mind to," that you've selected beforehand really helps with this.)

As a general rule, any thought that does not feel good is not true.

A quick note: It's easy to get in a war with your thoughts. That's not helpful. This isn't about resisting or fighting old thoughts, which only makes them stronger.

If you find yourself struggling to shift the thought, there are a few ways to respond. The first option is to feel any fear or pain underneath, asking yourself what you're afraid of.

You can also simply return to your breath. It helps to shift to neutral, which is simply centering into the present moment, before moving forward to embrace forward-thinking thoughts.

For today's prompt, start by energetically reconnecting to the feeling / vision of the person you want to be and the life you want to live. Soak in the energy of that vision.

Then, tune into the thoughts and beliefs this person has running through her mind all day long.

How does she see herself? How does she see the world? What does she expect? What does she feel confident and good about? What beliefs does she have about herself?

For example:

*I'm so excited to be creating things I love and making amazing money doing it. Everything is falling into place so easily. I have great relationships. People respect me. I respect myself. I know who I am and have clarity on what I want in life. There's always enough time to do everything that's important to me. My presence is valuable. The people in my life are lucky to have me, and I'm lucky to have them. My health and happiness are so important. I make sure to care for myself first because my energy is the fountain from which the rest of my life flows.*

As you connect to this expanded version of consciousness, the things you manifest in your daily life will, over time, reflect this energetic expansion. It's you, who you always were. The truth of who you are, minus the fear, doubt and past pain.

Now it's your turn! Write out the thoughts and beliefs that reflect the person you are now choosing to become. If you don't actually believe any of these things, you can create a transitional affirmation, something like, "I want to believe..." or, "I'm learning to believe."

_____

_____

_____

_____

_____

_____

_____

_____

_____

_____

_____

_____

_____

_____

_____

_____

_____

_____

---------------------------------------------------------------

---------------------------------------------------------------

---------------------------------------------------------------

---------------------------------------------------------------

---------------------------------------------------------------

---------------------------------------------------------------

---------------------------------------------------------------

---------------------------------------------------------------

---------------------------------------------------------------

---------------------------------------------------------------

---------------------------------------------------------------

---------------------------------------------------------------

---------------------------------------------------------------

---------------------------------------------------------------

---------------------------------------------------------------

---------------------------------------------------------------

---------------------------------------------------------------

---------------------------------------------------------------

---------------------------------------------------------------

---------------------------------------------------------------

---------------------------------------------------------------

---------------------------------------------------------------

---------------------------------------------------------------

---------------------------------------------------------------

---------------------------------------------------------------

---------------------------------------------------------------

---------------------------------------------------------------

# Day 26: What is your relationship to money?

Your relationship with money impacts your entire life. Money ranks high among reasons people stay in jobs, relationships and other situations that don't serve them.

How you relate to money affects how much you earn and enjoy, and how much struggle, worry and fear you experience, regardless of the quantity of money in your life.

You deserve to feel abundant. You deserve to receive a continual flow of money that supports your needs and desires. You deserve to feel safe and secure and like there's always enough.

You deserve to know that your gifts are worthy and valuable of divine compensation. You deserve to believe in your dreams and follow them while feeling financially supported and abundant. You can receive as much money as you desire. You are capable and worthy of receiving.

Right away, the first step is to journal out your immediate response to those statements. What's coming up for you? Do you feel like that would never be possible? Or that there will never be enough? Write it all down.

The second step is to ask — where did these beliefs came from? Connect to any painful memories you've had with money. Maybe growing up you felt like your needs were too much, or you felt afraid money would run out. Maybe you had more than others and felt used or bitchy or guilty for having more.

Maybe you experienced a moment where someone said it wasn't possible to earn money doing the thing you love, and you better be practical and get a secure job. (Even though jobs aren't really all that secure!)

Write it all down. Ask your higher self for help with seeing things differently. "My parents may have felt afraid the money was going to run out, but they were only running off programming they inherited. I'm sorry my younger self felt ashamed for wanting things my parents felt they couldn't afford. I'm ready to write a new story now and change my experience of having money."

Feel any feelings that come up to release these experiences from your physical body. (Try the meditation at SoulScrollJournals.com/bonuses to learn how to release your feelings.)

Then, connect to a new story. Ideas you'd rather believe. Some to play with include: Money is an infinite resource that can't run out. (Even if your current supply dwindles, you can always create channels for more to flow in your life. Billions of dollars are always circulating.)

Rich people are fake, selfish or bitchy. (Plenty of rich people are kind and generous! You will be a kind, real and generous wealthy person.)

It's safe to receive with joy, gratitude and ease. (You don't have to feel guilty about having money. When you allow yourself to fully receive abundance, you are able to help others.)

This is a big topic, but today, write out your fears and doubts and limiting beliefs around money. Ask where they came from. And shift to a new story.

What would you like your relationship with money to be? Maybe you'd like to appreciate the flow in your life more and feel supported by it, or capable of receiving enough to support your needs and desires.

Maybe you'd like to know in your heart that you are capable of creating financial freedom, whatever that looks like for you. What does that look like?

Perhaps you'd like to acknowledge money's important role in your life with a sense of love and appreciation rather than fear or guilt. If you've done this before, it's always good to shift again. Dive in!

_____

_____

_____

_____

_____

_____

_____

_____

_____

_____

_____

_____

_____

_____

_____

_____

----------------------------------------

----------------------------------------

----------------------------------------

----------------------------------------

----------------------------------------

----------------------------------------

----------------------------------------

----------------------------------------

----------------------------------------

----------------------------------------

----------------------------------------

----------------------------------------

----------------------------------------

----------------------------------------

----------------------------------------

----------------------------------------

----------------------------------------

----------------------------------------

----------------------------------------

----------------------------------------

----------------------------------------

----------------------------------------

----------------------------------------

----------------------------------------

----------------------------------------

----------------------------------------

----------------------------------------

# Day 27: What is your relationship to your inner guidance?

Living a soulful life is very much about connecting within, hearing the desires of your heart, asking for guidance with the next right steps and taking them, with faith.

The problem is we're taught to look outside of ourselves for advice and distrust our inner voice. We're taught that people older than us and authority figures like doctors, teachers, religious figures or parents know what's best for us more than we know what's best for us.

This couldn't be further than the truth. You are your own greatest authority. Your heart knows how to discover your unique genius and how to create the extraordinary life you're meant for.

The energy that flows through you as consciousness is the same energy that created the world. Your connection to that intelligence is what will allow you to blossom in the exact perfect way you're meant to.

Many things block you from hearing this voice. Fear. Repressed emotion. False ideas that others know better than you or that asking for everyone's opinion is a good thing. Spending too much time on social media, focusing on others' lives and possibilities rather than your own.

Listening to your inner guidance isn't always easy because your intuition will lead you down unconventional paths that test your faith. Your conscious mind can't always understand why or how it will all work out.

Your inner guidance will tell you to do things that don't make logical sense, but that's okay. It doesn't have to make sense. It just has to make you happy. Your sense of excitement and joy lets you know you're on the right path.

Because of these old habits and ways of seeing the world, many people write off their inner guidance and stop listening.

This results in you creating a life out of alignment with who you really are. This in turn causes emotional pain, which most people judge, repress and deny, thinking they're wrong for feeling it — I *should* be happy! — but resisting this pain only blocks the very wisdom from your heart that's trying to help you find your way back home.

Your heart / soul / gut never stop speaking to you, but the voice can become so quiet underneath layers of fear and repressed emotions that it becomes hard to hear.

To reclaim this connection, first set the intention. Then start asking your inner self for help with small decisions. What should you eat for breakfast? What does your soul want to wear?

What should you do with a free afternoon? Maybe it's clean the house. But maybe your soul wants to go for a bike ride, even if your bike has layers of dust on it and flat tires.

Reclaim your connection. Listen to it. This voice will show you exactly how to uncover your unique genius and give it to the world, one right next step at a time. Nobody else can do this for you, but you. Your extraordinary life rides on your willingness to find the courage to listen to the voice within.

Today, investigate your relationship with your inner guidance.

Who do you look to as an authority or for guidance? In what ways are you making your inner voice hard to hear?

Where in life *do* you listen to this voice? What would you need to believe to follow this voice in all areas? What message does this voice have for you today? Journal below!

_____

_____

_____

_____

_____

_____

_____

_____

_____

_____

_____

_____

_____

_____

_____

_____

_____

_____

_____

_____

_____

_____

_____

_____

_____

_____

_____

_____

_____

_____

_____

_____

_____

_____

_____

_____

_____

_____

_____

_____

_____

_____

_____

_____

_____

_____

_____

_____

_____

_____

_____

# Day 28: What is your relationship to failure and disappointment?

Living an extraordinary life requires us to face failure and disappointment with strength and bravery. It's easy to feel courageous and excited at the start. But too often people give up at the first sign of failure or discomfort, telling themselves stories about how what they want isn't possible.

Social messages tell us failure is something to fear, or that making mistakes is bad. Many people suffer from perfectionism, feeling like making an error means they can't do anything right.

But mistakes are good. They mean you're growing and stretching out of your comfort zone. It's important to learn from them of course, but without trial and error, there would be no victory.

Thomas Edison failed 1,000 times before creating the first lightbulb, but he always remained devoted to his vision. He succeeded because he didn't give up. He failed more than he succeeded! But his successes were so significant that his name will be repeated forever.

Failure isn't opposite to success; it's part of success. You can't succeed unless you fail! Each time you learn something new. Each missed mark is an opportunity to renew your vision and dig deeper to become the person you were born to be.

This is very important because how you respond to life's low moments defines how high you rise. Without gaining the ability to bounce back from life's low moments, you'll never be able to taste the sweetness of success waiting for you if you just keep going.

It's important to note that we must learn from failure. Sometimes you may feel called to change course or adjust the path in pursuit of your goal. Maybe the universe is guiding you to a better-aligned pathway. Everything is always working in your favor.

When things go wrong, it's easy to try and force or control. It's easy to disconnect from your body and retreat into your head where anxious, sad or fearful thoughts take over.

I've found the best way to move through these times is to tune into my heart and process my emotions — even though everything in me wants to numb out with technology. I love using oracle cards and journaling as ways to reconnect not only to myself, but to the universe. Once reconnected, I renew my vision, see if anything needs to shift, and ask for guidance on how to move forward.

Your heart is always speaking to you, sending you ideas and visions intended to move you forward in life. But clinging to the pain of the past, ideas of how things should be and stories about how nothing is working out for you will block you from receiving those insights.

Today is all about clearing any past disappointments and reshaping your relationship with failure so you can become unstoppable.

First, consider any past disappointments weighing on your heart. What are you afraid they say about who you are or what's possible for you? What do you need to know that will let you move on? Repeat this affirmation to yourself every time you feel caught up in ideas of how things should be.

Next, identify any lessons or blessings that came from past disappointments. Connecting to how they grew you or ended up working in your favor will help you re-shape your response to future disappointments.

Then examine your relationship to disappointment itself. In what ways do you fear it? How can you see it differently? How would you like to respond in the future when you feel disappointed or like you failed? What beliefs will help cement this shift? What does your higher self want you to know about any obstacles or challenges you may encounter?

Journal below.

_____

_____

_____

_____

_____

_____

_____

_____

_____

_____

_____

_____

_____

_____

_____
_____
_____
_____
_____
_____
_____
_____
_____
_____
_____
_____
_____
_____
_____
_____
_____
_____
_____
_____
_____
_____
_____
_____
_____
_____
_____
_____
_____

## Integration

You made it! Congratulations on all the work you've done over the past four weeks.

These next two days are an important time to review and integrate the shifts you've made so they will not only last, but deepen over time.

## 29: What have been the biggest realizations and shifts for you over the past four weeks?

We're in the final two days of the Design Your Life Workbook! Be so proud of yourself for showing up and committing to this process.

It doesn't matter if you skipped days or even skipped around. What matters is that you showed up, took time for yourself, and committed to expanding into the next level of you.

You've shifted old, stagnant energy and shed light on beliefs blocking you from manifesting your desires. You've created new thoughts and beliefs that will support your journey of creating an extraordinary life.

And you've created new habits, even if those habits aren't fully engrained into your being — which is why today's work is so important.

Take a moment to feel good about all the work you've done!

Digging deep like you have, facing things that may have felt painful and finding the courage to take responsibility for your life so you can change it is no small feat.

Many people don't do this work and that's why most people don't love their lives! It takes time to truly integrate these shifts at the deepest levels — time way beyond these two days.

But this is a good start to creating awareness of the exact ways you've shifted and the most important takeaways you want to integrate into your life going forward.

This is important because it's easy to forget things. Think of the most life-changing book you've read. While you remember the basic gist, you probably forget the specifics.

If you were to read the book again, it would probably seem like a new book.

By taking time to reflect on your journey, and connecting to a handful of ideas, beliefs or epiphanies you want to continually remind yourself of, you can begin the work of truly integrating these shifts into your entire life.

Without doing this work, it's easy to unconsciously return to beliefs and habits that don't serve you and reinforce a life that doesn't make you happy.

To allow yourself the gift of evolution requires an ongoing commitment to maintain these changes and keep expanding into new ones.

With that in mind, here are a few questions to consider:

What shifts, ah-has or epiphanies have been the most powerful for you?

What was the biggest identity shift you had over the past four weeks, as in how you think of yourself as a person? What do you want to lock in there?

What was the biggest limiting belief you shed that you want to stay conscious of as you move on?

What have you released that once felt so heavy? What are you feeling ready or excited for?

How do you feel now compared to when you began?

What else are you thinking and feeling? If you're needing to shift anything, feel free to do that below, too.

Simply write out whatever's on your mind and invite in a higher perspective from your soul. It's always there, always waiting.

_____

_____

_____

_____

_____

_____

_____

_____

_____

_____

_____

_____

_____

_____

_____

_____

_____

_____

_____

_____

_____

_____

_____
_____
_____
_____
_____
_____
_____
_____
_____
_____
_____
_____
_____
_____
_____
_____
_____
_____
_____
_____
_____
_____
_____
_____
_____
_____
_____

# 30: What do you need to keep this momentum going?

Over the past 30 days, you've connected to big dreams, visions and ideas of who and what you want to become.

You've felt the thrill of feeling like anything was possible.

Know that the secret to maintaining this feeling and manifesting the big dreams in your heart lies in your daily habits.

Today I invite you to get more specific and commit to new habits or ways of being that will support you as you move on.

Tap into the energy of your higher self or the future you and ask — what habits can you incorporate daily to maintain this energy or move toward your goals?

That might include continuing to journal as a daily practice. (Maybe another Soul Scroll Journal calls to you!)

Maybe you'd like to make a commitment to fitness or healthy eating to nurture your energy and help your aura buzz with aliveness. Get specific here, outlining the exact activity and when you will do it.

For example, maybe you want to focus on eating healthy lunches, and will take time each Sunday to plan your meals ahead for the week. Start small and set yourself up for success.

Perhaps you'd like to try something new like dancing or painting or pottery to stoke the fire of your creativity. Commit and then actually do it!

If you'd like support, grab SSJ's Play with the Day yearly goal journal, which offers monthly goal setting and daily habit tracking.

Other ideas include starting a daily meditation practice, taking time to work on a passion project or finally starting your new business idea.

Maybe you simply want to stay aware of your self talk and will keep learning about empowering new beliefs that support the life you want to create.

No matter where your exploration takes you today, end with this:

If you could bottle up a message from how you feel now to your future self, what would that message be?

Feel free to read this message whenever you're feeling lost or down, or need to reignite your excitement on the path forward.

Explore below!

_____
_____
_____
_____
_____
_____
_____
_____
_____
_____
_____
_____

# The end!

Thank you so much for choosing Soul Scroll Journals as a guide through the galaxy of your inner world!

Our mission is to help you understand yourself so you can create a life as unique as you are.

We hope that you now feel more empowered to create a beautiful life of your choosing rather than the one you're programmed for or expected to live.

Please let us know how your experience was!

## What's next:

**1. Leave a review.**

Did you love this journal? Share your thoughts on Amazon and let others know about your experience so their lives can also be transformed. This is how we change the world!

**2. Download your bonus gifts at SoulScrollJournals.com/ bonuses.**

If you haven't already downloaded the Feeling Awareness meditation to help you connect to your heart and release painful emotions, go do that now!

**3. Join the Soul Scroll Journal Family Facebook group!**

Head to www.facebook.com/groups/soulscrolljournals to connect with others also on the path of creating an extraordinary life.

## About Soul Scroll Journals

Everyone has a dream inside of them they're meant to live. Yet not everyone trusts themselves enough to create this dream and realize their destiny.

This is no small thing. The unique essence of you was created for a reason, and it will never exist again.

Too many people are held back because they don't know how to release past pain, find the answers within, and trust themselves to create the extraordinary life they're meant to live.

Too many people are so full of external information and well-meaning but ultimately noisy advice that they've lost connection to their own hearts.

We wanted to inspire dreamers to put down their phones and scroll their souls.

To find the vision within and connect to the heartfelt guidance to create it, one day at a time.

That's why Soul Scroll Journals were born. The journals are your friend and unbiased guide to help you connect to your heart, clarify your dreams and desires, and teach you how to use your intuition to create it.

They'll help you become the person you were always meant to be — right now.

Download a free, powerful meditation to release past pain and connect to your heart at SoulScrollJournals.com/bonuses.

Made in the USA
San Bernardino, CA
03 March 2020

65256752R00083